Ancient Civilizations Uncovered

Decoding Secrets of the Past

Table of Contents

Chapter 1. Introduction

Delve into the enigmatic world of our ancestors through our fascinating Special Report, "Ancient Civilizations Uncovered: Decoding Secrets of the Past." Prepare to journey back in time, traversing centuries, and navigating through the captivating stories of long-lost cultures. This report meticulously pieces together the arcane lore of once flourishing societies – from the megalithic marvels of Stonehenge to the architectural masterpieces of the Mayans. Set on this thrilling exploration, we promise you'll unravel secrets intertwining history and mystery, genius and grit. Captivating narratives coupled with stunning visuals bring the majestic past alive, right to the comfort of your favorite reading nook. Both hobbyists and history buffs will find a goldmine of information - rich, enlightening, and surprisingly accessible. With each page you turn, you'll find another reason that makes this special report worthy of being a prized possession!

Chapter 2. Unveiling the Hushed: Discovering Hidden Ancient Cities

Human civilization, over millennia, has birthed myriad cities, beacons of wealth, culture, and power that have stood the test of time. However, others hidden beneath the earth's surface and the vast oceans speak vivid tales of thriving cultures that mysteriously vanished without a trace. Inherent within the echoes of these lost cities are secrets veiled in obscurity, waiting to be unearthed, to whisper once more the stories of their existence, their peak, and their ultimate decline.

2.1. The Mysterious Halls of Petra

Situated amidst the deserts of modern-day Jordan, the 'lost' city of Petra thrived in the shadows of towering red rock cliffs. It was rediscovered in 1812 by Swiss explorer Johann Ludwig Burckhardt who, clad as an Arab scholar, penetrating the secrecy surrounding the city.

Descending gradually from the arid wilderness, one would first set eyes on Al-Khazneh, the Treasury. Carved entirely from the rosy-pink sandstone cliff, its detailed Greek-influenced architecture and urn-topped façade are no less than an awe-inspiring spectacle. It is a testament to the ingeniousness of the Nabataeans, who conceived Petra, that splendid city in the sand, around the 6th century BC, turning it into an important crossroads for trade. They not only constructed complex water control systems but adapted to the harsh environment, excelling in art, culture, and commerce.

Bit by bit, archaeologists are revealing the stories buried within the city's spectacular ruins. From evidence of Nabataean knowledge in advanced pottery to the city's decline post-Roman acquisition, understanding Petra's secrets is akin to assembling an intricate jigsaw puzzle from the echoes of the past.

2.2. Lost and Found: Pompeii

Unlike Petra, Pompeii's fall was sudden, brutal, and natural. In AD 79, the deadly eruption of Mount Vesuvius froze this bustling metropolis— a prosperous port city of the Roman Empire— in time. Carbonized bread in bakery ovens, wall paintings frozen in mid-brushstroke, and the petrified bodies of inhabitants, forever captured in their final moments, provide a hauntingly vivid glimpse into the everyday life of ancient Romans.

Rediscovered in 1748, Pompeii has provided archaeologists a wealth of knowledge about Roman culture, administration, architecture, and more. One of the most startling discoveries was the city's complex water and sewage system that rivaled any modern city. Graffiti, found etched often humorously and sometimes crudely on walls, echoes societal and political commentary of the time, cementing its resonance with a modern reader. Pompeii, until today, keeps blurring the divide between the ancient and modern, contributing to our discernment of the rich tapestry of life in a Roman city.

2.3. Mahendraparvata: A Forgotten Empire in the Jungle

Delving into Cambodia's verdure-drenched wilderness, we stumble upon the enigmatic ruins of Mahendraparvata. Often overshadowed by the more famous Angkor Wat, this 1,200-year-old city had been a thriving capital of the early Khmer empire. Rediscovered in 2012, using an innovative LiDAR technology that unravels hidden features beneath dense forest canopy, Mahendraparvata served as a vital link between understanding the societal complexities and the eventual dominance of the Khmer empire.

Scripts inscribed on sandstone blocks, wasted waterways, and remnants of countless temples stand as mute witnesses to the city, believed to be one of the first instances of large scale city planning in human history. The city's elaborate roadways and reservoir systems and the transformative influence of Hindu cosmology on the city's development leaves modern archaeologists and historians in awe of the complex society that once thrived here.

The world of our ancestors is filled with fascinating stories of grandeur and genius, revealed one artifact, one inscription, or one archaeological excavation at a time. The discovery of these hidden cities, these buried testimonies of progress and prowess, emphasizes the remarkable resilience and innovative spirit inherent in human beings, regardless of the epoch they inhabit. As we unravel their secrets and learn from them, these cities stand not just as remnants of a bygone era, but tangible symbols of our shared history and enduring human legacy.

Chapter 3. Artifacts of Antiquity: A Tangible Link to the Past

In the hushed corridors of time, artifacts stand as the tangible, surviving vestiges of civilizations long extinct. Fashioned from stone, bone, clay, and metal, these objects of antiquity whisper tales of human enterprise, genius, and history, providing us a physical link to our ancient past.

3.1. The Material World of Our Ancestors

Every artifact, whether a splendid golden crown or a simple pottery shard, offers a window into the culture that crafted it. These objects bear with them codes of societal norms, religious beliefs, and technological prowess, allowing us to perceive civilizations of bygone eras in the framework of their own creation. Delving deep into the traces of their material culture, we can unearth essential keys for discerning their customs, values, and technologies that influenced the course of human chronicle.

3.2. Stone-Borne Stories

Stone tools and sculptures form a significant portion of the archaeological record. From ancient stone axes to the renowned Rosetta Stone, the messages conveyed by these silent witnesses are priceless.

The hand axes of the Acheulean era, which came into existence nearly 1.76 million years ago, mark the advent of the first significant innovation in stone tool technology. These teardrop-shaped tools used by Homo erectus were a testament to their increasing brain size and evolving manual dexterity.

Contrast that with the Rosetta Stone, a decree issued by Ptolemy V in 196 BC. Its trilingual inscription unlocked the mystery of ancient Egyptian hieroglyphics, radically shifting our understanding of a civilization that, until then, had been largely shrouded in mystery.

3.3. Metal Marks of Progress

The transition from Stone Age to Bronze Age marked an extraordinary leap in technological capability. Metallurgical advancements led to the creation of sophisticated tools, weapons, and ornamental items, reflecting the growing complexity of early societies.

The Nebra sky disk, unearthed in Germany, is an exquisite exemplar of Bronze Age artisanship. This celestial map from 1600 BC merges practical knowledge of seasons with religious iconography, offering profound insights into the minds of people who lived more than 3,500 years ago.

3.4. Echoes from Clay and Bone

Clay tablets, often overlooked due to their modest appearance, hold significant historical importance. Dating around 4,000 - 3,000 BC, Mesopotamian cuneiform tablets are the earliest known form of writing, the beginning of human record-keeping, and the birth of history.

Similarly, oracle bones from ancient China served multi-faceted roles. These ox scapulae and turtle plastrons were inscribed with early Chinese script and were used for pyro-osteomancy, a form of divination. This method of divine communication offers invaluable insights into the religion, politics, and social structure of the Shang Dynasty.

3.5. The Panorama Displayed in Pottery

A remarkable arm of archaeology is the study of pottery, vessels crafted primarily for utility, but implicitly, a canvas reflecting the aesthetics and technological progress of its maker. Each piece tells stories of origin, use, and eventual discardment, marking the life trajectory of the artifact itself.

The intricate Minoan pottery provides a fascinating outlook on the Bronze Age civilization of Crete, famed for their elaborate, vibrant frescoes telling tales of mythology and rituals. Contrastingly, the enigmatic Indus Valley civilization, one of the oldest urban centers globally, is renowned for its minimalist and utilitarian pottery, yielding glimpses into a society steeped in pragmatism.

3.6. Artifacts as Aids in Contextual Chronology

While artifacts reverberate the grandeur and creativity of ancient societies, they also serve a more mundane but critical role in establishing a chronological context. Radiocarbon dating and dendrochronology, alongside various other dating methods, have served to accurately contextualize archaeological findings and reconstruct credible timelines of humanity's saga.

For instance, the elaborately adorned 'Ötzi the Iceman,' discovered in the Italian Alps, and dated back to around 3300 BC, shed light on Copper Age Europeans' life. His tools, clothing, and even the content of his stomach have all significantly enriched our understanding of a hitherto unknown epoch.

As this examination of the past draws to an end, it is clear that each artifact, no matter how big or small, opulent or humble, stands as a testament to human ingenuity and the relentless march of progress. Their intrinsic capacity to connect us with our history, their silent narratives, and the enigma that shrouds them make these objects of antiquity enduringly tantalizing, forever beckoning us to dig deeper, and seek more.

Chapter 4. Ancient Architectural Grandeur: Marvelous Structures that Time Forgot

The primordial earth, barren of human-made structures, pulsated with raw, untouched beauty. The kaleidoscope of colors that painted the world ended at the horizon, not pinned down by concrete jungles or the incessant buzz of urban life. Yet, humans yearned to leave their indelible mark. Armed with the twin tools of imagination and resourcefulness, they set the foundation stones of an architectural legacy that time, in all its enduring majesty, forgot to erase.

4.1. The Colossal Creations of Egypt

The spectacle of the wave-like dunes of Egypt, accompanied by the blaring ball of fire in the sky, is jaw-dropping. More so, when you see the three colossal, geometrical structures – the Pyramids of Giza. Conceived as the final resting place of the Pharaohs, they were the culmination of Egypt's architectural prowess, where spirituality coalesced with architectural expertise.

In the Great Pyramid of Giza, just over 230m in length at the base, approximately 146m high, an estimated 2.3 million blocks of stone were used, each weighing an average of 2.5 to 15 tons. This architectural marvel, an epitome of precision, was constructed over two decades, showcasing the perseverance and shared vision of the people of this ancient civilization.

The Pyramids' grandeur, however, isn't merely a testament to the era's engineering prowesses. Inside, a labyrinth of hidden rooms and secret passageways unfolds, drowning onlookers with a sense of wonder and offering unique insight into their creators' minds.

4.2. The Mystifying Code of Stonehenge

Contrasting the Egyptian penchant for geometric precision is the mystifying Stonehenge on Salisbury Plain in England. This prehistoric monument, consisting of a ring of standing stones each around 4m high, 2m wide, and weighing approximately 25 tons, emits an air of inscrutability that has stirred the imagination of researchers for generations.

Many theories have been formulated, with one suggesting Stonehenge as a sacred burial ground due to human remains uncovered in the vicinity. Others posit it might have been an astronomical calendar, given that certain stones align with specific astronomical events, like the summer and winter solstices.

4.3. The Ornate Splendor of the Mayans

As we traverse the Atlantic and venture into Central America, we come across the Mayan civilization, equally memorable for its architectural grandeur. The Mayans were adept in many areas, including mathematics, astronomy, and writing. This knowledge profoundly influenced their architectural style – intricate, ornate, and cosmic.

The Kukulkan Pyramid at Chichen Itza, also known as El Castillo and reaching a height of 30m, exhibits their architectural finesse. Intricate carvings and glyphic inscriptions adorn the pyramid's stone, telling tales of their society, values, and beliefs. Twice in a year, during the Spring and Autumn equinoxes, the play of sun and shadow adorns the pyramid with the illusion of a serpent descending its steps, a display that has mesmerized onlookers for centuries.

4.4. The Enduring Legacy of the Romans

The Romans were admired for their remarkable civic sense, best embodied in their architectural achievements: aqueducts, bathhouses, amphitheatres, and temples. Their use of arches, concrete, and systematic town planning paved the way for many modern architectural practices.

The Colosseum, Rome's amphitheatre, was a fine example of their architectural capabilities. With a seating capacity of approx 50,000, it was a socially inclusive space where all Romans, regardless of stature, could attend functions. It illustrated how architecture was not merely about grandeur but also fostering societal ties and shared experiences.

4.5. Relevance in the Modern World

Ancient architecture is an invaluable inheritance, a testament to our ancestors' creativity and genius. Each stone, each monument, speaks volumes about who they were and what they believed in. As we explore them, we find not only forgotten structures but also a living, breathing narrative that prompts us to reflect and learn from the past to inform the present.

In the end, it's not just about marveling these structures but cherishing and preserving them for future generations. They remind us of a time when humans, amidst survival struggles, still found time and energy to create and leave their mark in the sands of time— a testament to human resilience, spirit, and capacity for greatness that encapsulates our collective journey as a species. The myriad tales they unfold whisper eternal truths—in every grain of sand, in every block of stone, there is a universe waiting to be discovered.

Chapter 5. Reconstructing Lost Languages: Deciphering Ancient Scripts

Ever since humanity started documenting their thoughts and experiences, languages have evolved with us. Our relationship with languages is an intricate tapestry of cultural nuances, historical periods, and sociopolitical dynamics. This chapter provides an all-encompassing exploration of how scholars have tirelessly reconstructed lost languages by deciphering ancient scripts.

Our first stop on this exploration begins with one of the most notable ancient scripts that led to significant advancements in understanding ancient civilizations — the Rosetta Stone.

5.1. The Rosetta Stone: The Key to Deciphering Egyptian Hieroglyphs

Discovered in 1799 during Napoleon Bonaparte's campaign in Egypt, the Rosetta Stone proved to be the key to unlock the secrets of the ancient Egyptian language and culture. It was inscribed with three scripts: Ancient Greek, Demotic, and Egyptian Hieroglyphs.

For scholars and historians, the ancient Greek text provided a clear understanding of the stone's content, which helped them make educated guesses about the corresponding Hieroglyphs. With relentless pursuit, it was Jean-François Champollion, a French linguist, who successfully deciphered the Hieroglyphs in 1822, consequently breathing new life into our understanding of this enigmatic civilization.

Moving east, we now take a look at the decipherment of a script that had cost several scholars their sanity.

5.2. The Harrowing Journey to Decode Linear B

Arthur Evans, British archaeologist and creator of the Knossos palace reconstruction, unearthed clay tablets in Crete bearing an enigmatic script, which he called Linear B. Decades later, Michael Ventris, an architect without any formal training in linguistics, successfully decoded Linear B.

Ventris used a revolutionary approach, applying the principles of grid-based codebreaking to Linear B — a method contrary to the then-popular belief that each symbol corresponds with an image or idea. His work astonishingly revealed that the script represented an early form of Greek. Uncovering this linguistic treasure provided essential insights into Mycenaean civilization.

Our expedition now goes farther back in time, to the world's earliest known writing system.

5.3. Cracking the Cuneiform: The Story of Sumerian and Akkadian

Sumerian Cuneiform and Akkadian text were scripts used by some of the earliest civilizations in Mesopotamia. Scholars at first found the process of deciphering them confounding. The breakthrough came when archeologists unearthed the Behistun Inscription in Iran. Just like the Rosetta Stone, the Behistun monument had translations of the same text in multiple languages, including Old Persian, which scholars could read.

By analyzing corresponding words and phrases in Old Persian and the unknown scripts, Sir Henry Rawlinson, a British soldier and scholar, successfully translated parts of the Behistun Inscription, thereby deciphering Akkadian and later Sumerian Cuneiform.

5.4. Conclusion

The enduring quest to resurrect long-forgotten languages is laborious, involving multidisciplinary efforts from linguists, anthropologists, historians, and cryptographers, among others. With each step forward in this pursuit, humanity builds a proverbial bridge to our past, reconnecting with our ancestors and the life they led. We bring ourselves closer to understanding our common human legacy, collectively narrated through the 'code' of lost languages.

Unraveling these scripts' complexities, we grasp an even deeper appreciation for our ancestors' sophisticated systems of communication. Their genius has not faded into obscurity but has merely been waiting for us to decode it, thus serving as timeless testaments to the human spirit's resilience and inventiveness.

While this chapter has shed light on the arduous process of deciphering and reconstructing lost languages, centuries-old puzzles remain unsolved, and numerous scripts still elude professionals' understanding. The undeciphered Indus Script from the ancient Indus Valley Civilization and the enigmatic Rongorongo script of Easter Island are examples of such unfinished linguistic puzzles.

These hold the promise of revealing an unknown world, a hidden chapter in our shared history. With countless scripts yet to decipher, the quest continues, each step leading us back into the annals of the past, giving us another opportunity to delve deeper into our ancestors' enigmatic world.

Chapter 6. Enigmatic Artistry: Interpreting Ancient Art and Symbolism

Understanding the complex realm of ancient art and symbolism requires diving deep into the psyche of our ancestors, connecting with their vibrant cultures, deciphering their languages, exploring their myths, and interpreting the meanings they ascribed to the world around them. Their art wasn't merely for aesthetic pleasure. It had profound religious, societal, and even political connotations that can provide us invaluable insights about their way of life. Let's start this enlightening journey, retracing the path of our evolutionary odyssey and unwrapping the mystery of ancient symbols and art.

6.1. The Prism of Perception:

Art changes as civilization evolves, reflecting the changing ethos of society. Similarly, ancient artwork represents a time when humans were taking their nascent steps towards civilization. Contrary to modern perception, ancient art wasn't just crude cave paintings and simple pottery. Artistic expression ranged from simplistic representations of local fauna to complex depictions of mythological concepts, beings and events.

Exploring ancient art is akin to peeling off layers of an onion. With each layer, we come closer to the core, unraveling intricate patterns, styles, and symbols embedded in the artwork. They reveal the collective consciousness and shared cultural narratives of the era they belonged to - offering a unique lens to peer into the forgotten chapters of our shared human heritage.

6.2. Symbols and Their Complexity:

Symbolism constitutes a significant aspect of ancient art. More often than not, ancient artists used extensively symbolic language to express complex ideas. One must remember that these symbols were intensely personal and deeply rooted in the cultural fabric of their respective societies.

Symbols were a medium for communicating religious beliefs, societal norms, and philosophical insights. They represented the contemporary collective consciousness and were imbued with profound meanings. For instance, the ancient Egyptian "Ankh" represented eternal life, reflecting the deep-rooted belief in afterlife culture prevalent in Egyptian society. Comparable was the case with the labyrinth symbol of the Minoans, the 'Maya Vision Serpent', and the Norse thunder-god 'Thor's hammer', each signalling unique aspects of their local cultures.

6.3. Unmasking Cave Treasures:

Cave art remains one of the most captivating expressions of ancient artistry. Portraits of animals, hunters, warriors, celestial objects, and even phantom-beings adorning the wall are windows to the earliest human consciousness. They intertwine fact with myth, blending tangible reality with the perceived metaphysical.

Examining the cave paintings of Lascaux in France, or the Aboriginal rock art of the Kimberly region, Australia, we can observe a high degree of artistic skill combined with striking realism, transcending their mere categorization as primitive.

6.4. Decoding Ancient Iconography:

Ancient civilizations masterfully employed iconography to record historical events, celestial observations, societal hierarchies, and spiritual beliefs. Let's take the example of the hieroglyphs of Egypt. Emerging as a sophisticated system of pictorial writing, hieroglyphs were intricate and filled with symbolic nuances.

On the other side of the globe, the Mayan civilization was developing a distinct but equally rich iconographic language. Their steles and temple walls were adorned with highly stylized images of deities, sovereigns, mythical creatures, and sacred narratives expressed in a combination of logographs and phonetic symbols.

6.5. Unveiling Sculpted Stories:

Ancient sculpture provides another fascinating aspect of the ancient artistic endeavour. Whether the magnificent statues of Egypt or India, the totemic sculptures of the indigenous Americans, or the finely-crafted figures of the Greeks and Romans, each narrates a captivating tale.

Sculptures were more than mere decorative elements. They stood for piety, reverence, commemoration, and often as marking territories. The colossal stone figures on Easter Island, for instance, serve as a testament to the sculptural prowess and societal complexity of the Rapa Nui people.

6.6. Art as an Expression of Sacred Geometry:

Our ancestors perceived the cosmos as a sequence of harmonic geometrical patterns. This belief is evident in their architectural feats, designs and artworks. From the geometric precision of pyramids to complex mandala designs, from labyrinthine motifs to precise alignment of megalithic structures with stellar constellations - the ancient civilizations integrated cosmological philosophy with artistry.

Moreover, understanding sacred geometry can help us understand ancient mythology. For example, Hindu and Buddhist art frequently bear circular mandala patterns, representing the cosmos and spiritual journey towards enlightenment.

6.7. To Conclude: Reverence for the Ancient Mystique:

Delving into ancient art and symbolism is a captivating journey, offering an intimate view into the cultures, beliefs, philosophies, fears, and hopes of our ancestors. It unravels the mysterious language of the ancients, breathing life into their silenced voices, and connecting us to our shared past. By interpreting the symbolic narratives and artistry of ancient civilizations, we contribute to the perpetuation of their indomitable spirit and preserve the continuity of human cultural heritage.

Through the wealth of their legacy, we realize the profoundness of our own existence - a realization that surfaces only when we recognize the relevance of the enigmatic artistry of the ancients.

Chapter 7. Occult Rituals and Beliefs: Exploring the Sacred and the Profane

Lurking deep within the labyrinth of civilization's memory are the remnants of occult practices, sacred rituals, and peculiar beliefs—an intriguing tapestry woven into the fabric of our shared history. This chapter is a comprehensive exploration of various forms of ancient occult rituals and beliefs, navigating through their origins, practices, significance, and how they influenced societies, not only spiritually but politically as well.

7.1. Origin of Occult Rituals and Beliefs

The birth of occult rituals and beliefs can be traced back to prehistoric times, where early humans sought to understand the world around them. Paleolithic cave paintings, left by early human societies, provide the first evidence of ritualistic practices. These primitive forms of worship evolved with the emergence of civilization. With time, they grew structurally complex, embodying the unending quest of humanity to make sense of the cosmos.

7.2. Ancient Egyptian Occultism: The Divine Connection

Our first journey is into the heart of the Nile Valley — ancient Egypt. Egyptians maintained a pantheon of gods, each controlling different aspects of existence. Many of their rituals were designed to propitiate these gods, an essential task for maintaining Ma'at, the cosmic balance. For instance, the Opening of the Mouth ceremony, performed to reanimate the deceased in the afterlife, is a prime example of this civilization's intricate rituals.

7.3. Secrets of the Mayan World: Communing with the Cosmic Forces

Next, we explore the Mayan civilization. Mayan occult practices centered around a complex cosmology, a unique calendar system, and propitiatory sacrifices—often bloody, to appease their deities. At the heart of these rituals was the sacred ball game, pok-a-tok, believed to depict the mythical journey of the Hero Twins in the Popol Vuh, their sacred narrative.

7.4. Gnostic Mysteries: Hidden Knowledge and Spiritual Ascension

Venturing into the realm of the Gnostics, we delve into their unique belief system that prioritized individual spiritual knowledge (Gnosis) over orthodox faith. Gnostic rituals, mainly comprising of sacraments such as baptism, eucharist, and chrism, emphasized spiritual ascension, thereby fostering a personal, experiential form of divinity.

7.5. Celts and Druids: The Sacred Groves

Our journey takes us north to the Celts, specifically the Druids. Druidic practices were highly symbolic and nature-centric, conducted in sacred groves, primarily oak forests. Notorious for their practice of human sacrifice, as documented by Julius Caesar, Druids performed intricate rituals during the solstices and equinoxes.

7.6. Ancient Persian Magi: From Rituals to Empires

Moving eastward, we encounter the Persian Magi, ancient Zoroastrian priests adept in occult practices. Their rituals often involved the Haoma sacrament, similar to the Vedic Soma. The Magi influenced not only spiritual but also political ideologies, forming an oligarchic structure that laid the foundation of the Persian Empire.

This exhaustive journey into the enigmatic realm of ancient occult rituals bears testimony to our ancestors' attempts to comprehend the cosmos and its various phenomena. These practices were much more than primitive superstitions. They were painstaking efforts at creating meaning and order in the human experience, attempts to connect temporal life to the infinity of the universe.

From an anthropological standpoint, these rituals offer profound insight into ancient civilizations' worldview. How they understood themselves, their surroundings, and the cosmos, significantly influenced the socio-cultural fabric of their societies. Hence, understanding these practices becomes instrumental in decoding the secrets of our past, leading us to a deeper understanding of our present.

As we continue to embark on this voyage, let this journey into the past spark a sense of wonder and curiosity for the inherited wisdom of our ancestors. For deep within these chapters of antiquity lie the roots of modern thought, like seeds sown centuries ago that continue to influence our perception of the cosmos.

In the narrative of history, these ancient rituals and beliefs hold a mirror to humanity's primal desires and fears. They showcase human intellect's boundless capabilities, capable of weaving complex cosmological networks interlacing the spiritual and temporal realms. As seekers in the enigmatic world of our ancestors, let us continue to unravel these intriguing mysteries of the past.

23

Chapter 8. Advancement Through Ages: Prehistoric Technology and Innovation

We begin our journey not with civilizations but at the dawn of mankind, a time often shrouded in mystery. Yet, it is from this primeval epoch that we first witness the embers of human creativity and resourcefulness, sparking inventions that forever changed the path of our species.

8.1. The Discovery of Fire

Of no lesser importance than the wheel or written language, the taming of fire stands as one of humankind's most remarkable achievements. Harnessing fire permitted our ancestors to venture into the predatory darkness, cook food to neutralize toxins, and brave the bitter cold of Ice Age winters.

Around 1.7 million years ago, hominids, such as Homo erectus, achieved a major milestone in human evolution with the discovery of this elemental force. Archaeological sites, such as those in Wonderwerk Cave in South Africa, suggest that our ancestors might have generated fire by striking pieces of pyrite against flint – a feat nearly as remarkable as the discovery itself.

However, the deliberate control and reliable production of fire took hundreds of thousands of years to perfect, not until the era of Neanderthals and Homo sapiens. Evidence from numerous archaeological sites dating back around 300,000 years shows a clear presence of hearths - a sign our ancestors had mastered this life-altering force.

8.2. Stone Tools: Shaping Our Destiny

If fire lit the spark of invention in our ancestors' minds, stone tools were the resulting blaze that transformed that spark into an unstoppable conflagration. Stone tools, a simple yet radical innovation, made it possible for our ancestors to impose their will upon the environment, reshape their surroundings, and exploit new resources.

The Oldowan industry, named after the Olduvai Gorge in Tanzania where the first such tools were found, existed for nearly a million years starting around 2.6 million years ago. Early hominids such as Homo habilis created tools from rocks through a process called knapping, striking the rock on another to create sharp flakes. These rudimentary tools were used for various functions, ranging from butchering meat to gathering plant foods.

Following the Oldowan came the Acheulean industry, characterized by hand axes. These more advanced tools started to show their prevalence around 1.7 million years ago. They were mainly created by Homo erectus, a species becoming more adept at manipulating their environment. Hand-axes were multifunctional tools, proving handy in digging, butchering, and woodworking.

8.3. The Domestication of Plants and Animals: A Paradigm Shift

The transition from hunter-gathering lifestyles to settled farming communities was arguably one of the most profound transformations in human history. This change, known as the Neolithic Revolution, occurred independently in several global locations around 10,000 BCE, heralding the end of the last Ice Age.

In the 'Fertile Crescent,' a region encompassing modern-day Iraq, Syria, Lebanon, Israel, Palestine, Jordan, Egypt, and parts of Turkey and Iran, wild wheat and barley started to be cultivated deliberately. Alongside this, the domestication of animals, including goats, sheep, and cattle, was started, marking a massive shift in human subsistence strategies.

Meanwhile, the early Chinese were cultivating rice, while in the Americas, maize, beans, and squash formed the foundation of complex civilizations that would later emerge. Domestication of animals also occurred, with dogs likely being the first tamed animal. This period also saw the invention of pottery—used for storage and cooking—spinning, and weaving.

8.4. Metallurgy and the Dawn of the Bronze and Iron Ages

The discovery of metalworking was yet another radical leap in our technological journey. Around 7,000 years ago, copper was first smelted and used to make tools and decorative items marking the beginning of the Chalcolithic or Copper Age.

Copper's relatively low melting point and availability in pure form on the Earth's crust made it an ideal starting point for early metallurgy. The successive Bronze Age began when early societies learned to alloy copper with tin, creating a much harder and more durable material—bronish.

Near the end of the third millennium BCE, in West Asia, smelting technologies were further applied to develop iron tools and weapons, leading us into the Iron Age. The production of this superior metal required much higher temperatures and complex techniques, showing a significant advancement in our ancestors' technological prowess.

Chapter 9. The Progression in Art, Culture, and Communication

As our ancestor's material world grew more sophisticated, so did their cognitive and artistic landscapes. Rising from simple pictorial engravings on cave walls and token systems, humans began to express themselves in more symbolic and abstract fashions, contributing to cultural and societal progress.

The evidence of prehistoric art, such as those depicted on the walls of Chauvet Cave in France, Lascaux in France, and Altamira in Spain, portrays a sense of aesthetic understanding among prehistoric people. Symbols, handprints, and intricate depictions of animals provide a rich insight into their interactions with nature and their cultural ethos.

The etchings and numbering systems on clay tokens from ancient Mesopotamian sites, dating back to around 8000 BCE, can be considered a precursor to written language. Over time, these systems grew in complexity and paved the way for the creation of cuneiform by the Sumerians around 3200 BCE, mankind's first known writing system.

The technological strides made by our ancestors during prehistoric times laid the foundation for the towering civilizations in their future. From basic stone tools to sophisticated metallurgy, from cave paintings to written language, each advancement pushed us a step further on the incredible journey of human progress.

"Advancement Through Ages: Prehistoric Technology and Innovation" paints a vivid picture of the relentless human spirit - never content, ever curious, always stretching the fringes of what's possible. Our ancestors' legacy is not just in the tangible artifacts they left behind, but also visible in our modern world's metaphoric skyline - a testament to the fact that we stand tall on the shoulders of giants.

Chapter 10. Communities and Cultures: Understanding Ancient Social Structures

Our journey commences from where humanity found its roots, in tribes of prehistoric times transitioning into complex societies, typically identified today as civilizations. We will peer into the enigmatic social structures, ingenious organizational norms, and manifold ways in which our ancients lived and thrived.

10.1. The Dawn of Communal Living

Let's first set our sights on the era when humans began to settle and live together. The advent of agriculture around 10,000 B.C., also known as the Neolithic Revolution, moved them from a nomadic hunting-gathering lifestyle to a settled agrarian one. The prolific Fertile Crescent was a wellspring for early settlements due to its rich, well-irrigated soil. In these nucleated settlements, cooperation became an essential component. Shared communities cultivated land, built common structures, and formed rudimentary government structures to manage resources, marking the first signs of organized social units.

10.2. The Emergence of Complex Societies: A Case Study of Mesopotamia

Travelling forward in time brings us to Mesopotamia around 3500 BC, often referred to as the "Cradle of Civilization." Settled between the Tigris and Euphrates rivers, this region fostered one of the first complex societies. Villages matured into cities, densely populated with mixed-use structures: housing, temples, and marketplaces all coexisted closely, necessitating more sophisticated social dynamics.

People were stratified into three primary classes: elites, commoners, and slaves. Elites, which included royalty and priesthood, held substantial power and influence. Commoners, often responsible for farming, served as the backbone of the economy. Slaves, usually captives from raids or wars, performed menial tasks and carried the infrastructure's load.

10.3. Organizing Society: Egypt as an Example

By 3150 BC, Egypt had started to flourish as a civilization along the Nile's fertile banks. Primary dimensions of their societal structure revolved around the Pharaoh at its apex. They built life around the notion of "Maat," embodied harmony, justice, and righteousness, embracing these principles in their rule and daily living.

Egyptians engineered a centralized system of governance, primarily unitary and authoritarian. The Pharaoh was looked upon as divine, an intermediary between the gods and people. Subsequently, the Vizier, the high priest, and nobles who held different administrative, religious, and military roles assisted him.

10.4. Ancient Greek City-States: Introducing Democracy

On the crossroads of Europe, Asia, and Africa was the civilization of ancient Greece. This civilization consisted of independent city-states, each with its own government and laws. Athens, Sparta, and Corinth were the most prominent among them.

Singular in its societal setup than most ancient cultures, Athens was the birthplace of democracy around the 5th century BC. It provided its male citizens the right to participate in the assembly, voice their opinions, and vote. On the other hand, Sparta was a militaristic society with a dual monarchy and a strictly regimented citizen class.

10.5. The Castes of Ancient India

As a kaleidoscope of varied cultures and traditions, ancient India evolved a unique social stratification system called the Caste system. Rooted in the "Varna" system detailed in sacred texts, it divided people into four primary categories: Brahmins (priests), Kshatriyas (warriors), Vaishyas (traders), and Shudras (laborers). This societal division was hereditary and occupation-based, profoundly impacting social dynamics over time.

10.6. Examining the Feudal System of China

China, one of the world's oldest civilizations, was ruled by dynasties. The ancient Chinese societal structure was predominantly agricultural and feudal; land was distributed among the nobles, who then oversaw peasants' work on their land. At the pyramid's apex was the Emperor, revered as the "Son of Heaven."

In Conclusion:

Though diverse in norms and practices, these ancient social structures led to the complex societies we witness today. Lessons from the past offer insights about humanity's resilience and our ability to organize ourselves for the broader good. They serve as poignant reminders of human ingenuity, adaptability, and machinations shaping our collective journey so far, and those which will shape our voyage henceforth.

Chapter 11. Food from the Fabled Times: Recreating Ancient Cuisines

The human culinary journey comprises a vast time-spanning narrative pocked by a variety of tales. Whether it be the nutritional strategies of early hominids or the decadent feasts loved by ancient royalty, food customs have always served as an insightful lens for understanding our forebears.

11.1. Unearthing the Origins of Culinary Delights

Our primitive ancestors' diet mainly comprised foraged plants and hunted game, evolving based on availability. Rather than detailed recipes, food was prepared with simple techniques borne out of necessity. The utilization of fire, arguably the first human innovation in food preparation, dates back nearly 1.9 million years. Early Homo erectus discovered that cooked food had a multitude of advantages – it became safer, easier to digest, and tastier.

Evidence of these early food practices can be found in various archaeological sites worldwide. Carbonized remnants of plant matter like seeds and roots, fragmented bones and shells, coupled with remnants of ancient hearths, depict an intriguing panorama of our ancestors' diets, substantiating theories about the evolution of human dietetics.

11.2. Delectable Delicacies from the Mesopotamian Meadowlands

Mesopotamia, often dubbed the cradle of civilization, was also a fermenting ground for culinary traditions. Early inscriptions on clay tablets, the earliest form of written communication, reveal recipes dating back to the 18th century BCE.

People predominantly consumed barley, which was a staple grain, often made into flatbreads or beer. Beer, a significant element in rituals and daily meals, was deemed the gift of the gods. Other grains like wheat, emmer, and spelt also were used along with lentils, chickpeas, and a medley of fruits and vegetables.

11.3. Egyptian Gastronomical Grandeur

The bountiful Nile blessed the Egyptians with a plentiful supply of grains, fish, and fowl, paving the way for a varied and nourishing diet. Their staple, bread, was commonly prepared in conical molds or hand-shaped into flat loaves. Meals were often supplemented by vegetables grown in the fertile Nile delta.

A salient feature of Egyptian cuisine was its ubiquitous use of garlic, onions, and leeks. The Egyptians were also the pioneers of brewing beer and winemaking, a tradition that has since been globally appreciated.

11.4. The Culinary Canvas of the Indus Valley

The Indus Valley civilization, one of the oldest urban civilizations, had certain distinguishing culinary elements. Houses were designed with dedicated kitchen areas and stored jars of grains, affirming the centrality of food.

Archeological excavations in the region unearthed burnt rice grains, suggesting its widespread use. It was likely consumed with lentils, mustard, sesame, and a host of vegetables. Animals like humped zebu cattle, pigs, and water buffalo were probably part of their diet. Further, the usage of various spices like cumin, coriander, mustard, and fennel seemed quite prevalent, hinting at the warm, aromatic flavors that still dominate Indian cuisine.

11.5. The Mediterranean Marvel: Greek and Roman Dining Decadence

Both Greek and Roman civilizations were remarkable for their robust eating cultures. Greek cuisine centered around the "Mediterranean triad" - wheat, olive oil, and wine. They feasted on a variety of fresh vegetables, herbs, legumes, and fruits. Their meals were often accompanied by an assortment of cheeses.

Rome's culinary scene evolved dramatically over time. Initially adopting a simple diet, their repertoire expanded during the Empire era, morphing from frugal sustenance into lavish feasts. Their food was characterized by a mix of rustic flavors from farro (an ancient grain), olives, and legumes, to the opulence of garum - a salty fermented fish sauce.

11.6. Mayan Maize and More

For the Mayans, food was not just sustenance but a vital part of their religious and social fabric. Maize was considered a divine plant and formed the backbone of the Mayan diet. It was ground into dough (masa), which was used to make tortillas and tamales. They supplemented their meals with beans, squash, sweet potatoes, and a variety of fruits and vegetables.

The Mayans were also the pioneering chocolatiers, producing the first known chocolate drinks. Hunting and fishing provided them with additional protein sources.

It's fascinating to imagine these ancient culinary traditions being practiced, the aromas permeating through their abodes, and the conversations around their dining spaces. These historical insights offer a mesmerizing journey into the past, and through recreating these ancient cuisines, we keep their memory alive, honoring their legacy one bite at a time.

Chapter 12. Legacy of the Lost: How Ancient Civilizations Shape the Modern World

Our chronicle begins in an epoch, where thousands of years ago, the first civilizations were just beginning to form. These early societies, from the mighty Egyptians and indomitable Greeks to the enigmatic Mayans and industrious Chinese, were creators of a legacy - a legacy that not only explains our yesteryears but shapes our todays and tomorrows. Isn't it fascinating how much we still lean on philosophies, inventions, and cultural influences conceived millennia ago?

12.1. Mighty Egypt: Innovation Hub of the Ancient World

Few ancient civilizations have left a legacy as profound as that of the Egyptians. The seeds sown in the fertile lands surrounding the mighty Nile continue to bear fruit in present times. They introduced mankind to large-scale construction (the Pyramids being the most celebrated example), formulated one of the earliest known written scripts, Hieroglyphs, and made remarkable strides in mathematics, geometry, and medicine.

Their knowledge of geometry laid the foundation for modern land surveying, critical in today's construction and real estate industries. Medicine was practiced with such rigour and institutionalized learning that many consider Ancient Egypt as the cradle of healthcare. Egyptian physicians, some of whose names we still remember, were pioneers in surgery, gynecology, and pharmacology.

Today, we owe every diagnostic procedure, every antibiotic pill, and every surgical intervention, at least in part, to these ancient innovators.

12.2. Greek Intellect: Birthing Philosophy and Democracy

The civilization of Ancient Greece, with its pantheon of gods, epic literature and renowned city-states, radiates a unique glow in the annals of history. The Greeks' real inheritance, however, resides in their intellectual and political legacy. Philosophy, democracy, and critical thinking were their gifts to the world, concepts that continue to shape contemporary societies.

Rooted deeply in modern governance systems, the concept of democracy first saw light in the Athens City-State. In modern times, the world's most influential states run on models directly inspired by this ancient creation, with citizens playing pivotal roles in shaping their own societies.

12.3. Indus Valley: Metropolis and Trade Masters

The Indus Valley Civilization, also known as the Harappan Civilization, remains one of the most influential and mysterious civilizations of antiquity. Renowned for its urban planning and advanced sanitary systems, the civilization introduced the idea of a well-organized city-state with a standardized system of weights and measures, suggesting a highly developed trade system.

Modern-day urbanism is the progeny of the standards set by the Indus Valley Civilization, as are the systems of commerce and trade. Their planned cities with organized living spaces, communal baths, waste management systems - are concepts replicated in more sophisticated forms in today's urban areas.

12.4. Mayan Mastery: Astronomers and Architects

The Mayans, thriving in Central America, demonstrated astronomical prowess, developing a solar calendar that still stands the test of accuracy. Their unique step-pyramid architecture and extensive use of hieroglyphs leave a formidable mark in the world of design and communication. Buildings created by modern architects still retain the multidimensional essence and aesthetics inspired by Mayan master builders. The 365-day Haab solar calendar and the Lunar Series are clear reflections of the Mayans' profound understanding of celestial bodies. The Gregorian calendar, which wideworld uses, is built notably on Mayan mathematical applications.

In a broader context, it's hard to overstate the impact of these early cultures on our contemporary world. Logics of Ancient Greece, mixed with Mayan mathematics, seasoned with Egyptian medicine and served on an agrarian economy suggested by Mesopotamians, have had an enduring impact on the course of human progress.

Every colossal skyscraper, every democratic election, every city grid, every medical procedure links us with our admirable ancestors. They remind us that we, the modern population, are the bearers of a legacy uniquely human - a legacy of ceaseless innovation, relentless pursuit of understanding, and the infinite potential of the mind. We would indeed be irreverent not to appreciate how ancient civilizations convene in shaping the world we cherish today.